HOW TO PAY OFF YOUR MORTGAGE IN 5 YEARS

SLASH YOUR MORTGAGE WITH A PROVEN SYSTEM THE BANKS DON'T WANT YOU TO KNOW ABOUT

Disclaimer and FTC Notice

■ ■ ■

HOW TO PAY OFF YOUR MORTGAGE IN 5 YEARS

SLASH YOUR MORTGAGE
WITH A PROVEN SYSTEM THE BANKS DON'T
WANT YOU TO KNOW ABOUT

CLAYTON MORRIS
NATALI MORRIS

Your Free Gift

As a way of saying *thanks* for your purchase, we're offering a free PDF download that will help you pay off your house more quickly.

It's our HELOC Calculator.

Download it at:

https://goo.gl/cQgzp4

■ ■ ■

INTRODUCTION:

Chances are you picked up this book because you own a house and you're tired of making monthly mortgage payments. You're tired of working hard and never seeing any progress in paying down that massive debt. If this sounds like you then you've come to the right place.

This book can change your life.

It's not often an author can get away with saying something that bold. But in this case it's the truth because this strategy can free you from the oppression of your mortgage! When you're done reading this book you'll learn the exact strategies and tactics we used to pay off multiple mortgages in a few short years, saving hundreds of thousands of dollars. It's a strategy that NO bank will tell you about!

What you're about to discover is our step-by-step system for taking your 15 or 30-year mortgage and turning it into a 5 year mortgage. Moreover, we'll teach you about the mechanisms behind the different banking products and how some are meant to keep you buried in debt for decades. It's how the banks win and you lose.

Unlike those books that promise the world and fail to deliver, what you'll get is a blueprint that's both proven and achievable. We've got three kids and careers to worry about in our house so we know how valuable your time is. You don't have time to spend knee deep in finance books that leave you cross eyed. What you need, and what we will supply, is a straightforward plan that any busy person can implement to crush their primary mortgage.

We've outlined the process into a step-by-step system you can follow no matter how busy you are. In less than two months you will have everything in place to start paying off your mortgage. Obviously, results may vary depending on a variety of factors like the amount of your mortgage, your salary, credit score, etc. You'll get the blueprint but putting this into practice is up to you.

Before we get started, we want to invite you to dream about your life if you were mortgage free. How amazing would that feel!? How free would you be to travel, not worry about grocery bills, be more generous with your money! What would you do? What would that feel like!? Keep that wishful thinking in mind as you work towards that life by freeing yourself of the biggest expense in your life! Let's talk about how!

■ ■ ■

1

WHAT IS YOUR
MORTGAGE MADE OF?

The first step in beating your mortgage is to understand what it's made of. In this chapter we'll break out the most important pieces without getting in the weeds. The traditional mortgage is an octopus with multiple tentacles, some visible in plain sight and others hidden beneath the murky waters of the banking industry. Our job over the course of this book is to arm you with the tools you need in order to pay it off in no time.

The first time we secured a mortgage, we assumed that the monthly payments were made up of all kinds of fees, taxes, and bits and bobs. But if you look closely, it is not hard to see the anatomy of a mortgage. Let's break out some mortgage vocabulary to make sure you are crystal clear about what we are talking about.

Principal: This is the amount you borrowed. You needed $100,000 to buy a home? Surely your loan statement will have a number higher than $100,000 because of closing costs, filing fees, etc. Still $100,000 is the principal. It is the amount you asked the bank for.

Interest: We are going to discuss this in detail but in short: It is the amount of money you have agreed to pay in order to borrow the principal above. It is the rate of money for money.

Equity: Equity is the amount of value in the house that belongs to you. If your home is worth $200,000 and you don't owe any money on it, then you have $200,000 worth of equity in the home. That value is yours. But if you owe $100,000 on that $200,000 home, your equity is $100,000. This means that if you sold the house tomorrow for $200,000, you would pay the bank back $100,000 and keep $100,000. The $100,000 that you keep is your equity. It is your debt-free asset.

Taxes and Insurance: Every property will be taxed and you must have insurance on your property for any lender to consider taking the risk. Some lenders require that you add more money to your monthly payment so that they can keep it in an escrow account in order to pay the taxes and insurance for you. This adds to your monthly payment. I do NOT suggest you elect for one of these escrow accounts if you can avoid it. Some lenders do not make it an option. We will discuss this more later in this chapter.

PMI: If your lender considers your loan a little bit riskier than most, they may add an extra cost called Private Mortgage Insurance. For instance, say you can only put 10% of the purchase price in a down payment and you are asking the bank to pay for 90%. They consider you a riskier borrower. Say you have had a previous foreclosure or stain on your credit. They consider you a riskier borrower. Your PMI may disappear once your loan value is below 80% of the property value. It may not. The point is that this is a fee. It does not pay down your principal. It is money for the bank for taking a risk on you.

Those are the major components of a mortgage. Now let's really dig into the biggest beast on your mortgage statement: interest.

What is Interest?

Interest is simply the cost of borrowing money. It is typically paid back to a lender at a regular monthly interval. Interest is based on principal, or rather is calculated based on the amount you have asked to borrow.

For the purposes of our discussion, mortgage interest rate is tied to an annual percentage rate and that means that you're paying interest every month on the unpaid balance of your loan. Still owe $100,000? Then you're paying interest on $100,000 each month even if what you initially borrowed was more.

Interest on a mortgage can come in different shapes and sizes. Let's go over the most common types.

Interest Only Loans. These are exactly what they sound like: a mortgage that has a monthly payment that includes only interest. This means that every time you make a mortgage payment, none of that money goes to pay down your principal balance. It is a payment to the lender only. The principal balance of your loan goes untouched. So if you borrowed $100,000 and have been making interest-only payments for 5 years, your principal balance is still $100,000 because you agreed that your payments would not touch principal.

Why would someone agree to these unfavorable terms? In short: because it makes the monthly payments lower. There are sometimes reasons to do this but they are beyond the scope of this book. For the most part, interest-only is not a good deal. We have learned this the hard way.

During the 2009 mortgage collapse many homeowners had short-term balloon mortgages that were suddenly coming due. These were interest-only mortgages with a balloon note attached. A balloon note means that the principal balance will be due in full after a certain amount of time. It is a big bulk of money due at one time, which you can visualize like a balloon. These notes were popular in 2004 because they let homeowners get into a nice home for a low monthly payment and no money down. Unfortunately these homeowners did not understand their mortgages. At all! When they owed the full principal at the end of a short period of time and the value of the house had plummeted, they were in some weeds.

Maybe some of these homeowners had a goal to refinance these loans into amortized mortgages. We'll give them the benefit of the doubt because that sounds like a nice plan but it was 2009 and everything collapsed. That $100,000 house plummeted to $80,000 in value overnight. Homeowners lost jobs and still had loans out for the principal of $100,000 with the clock ticking towards that balloon. It was a really sad time.

Amortized Loans: Amortization by definition is the paying off of a debt according to a fixed schedule. Okay, what does that mean?

When you amortize a loan, you pay for interest and principal inside of a recurring payment. At the beginning of the loan, you are paying a lot of interest in that payment. As the balance goes down, the amount of interest you are paying is based on that principal that you are chipping away at.

Look at this sample amortization schedule from Bankrate.com on a $200,000 mortgage. Notice the monthly payment never changes but each payment has a different amount of interest, which is just the profit the bank makes from taking a risk to lend you that money, and principal, which is the amount you asked for to buy your house. Slowly you pay less interest over time because the interest is based on the dwindling principal balance.

DATE	PAYMENT	PRINCIPAL	INTEREST	TOTAL INTEREST	BALANCE
July 2017	$954.83	$288.16	$666.67	$666.67	$199,711.84
Aug. 2017	$954.83	$289.12	$665.71	$1,332.37	$199,422.73
Sept. 2017	$954.83	$290.09	$664.74	$1,997.12	$199,132.62
Oct. 2017	$954.83	$291.06	$663.78	$2,660.89	$198,841.57
Nov. 2017	$954.83	$292.03	$662.81	$3,323.70	$198,549.54
Dec. 2017	$954.83	$293.00	$661.83	$3,985.53	$198,256.54
Jan. 2018	$954.83	$293.98	$660.86	$4,646.38	$197,962.57
Feb. 2018	$954.83	$294.96	$659.88	$5,306.26	$197,667.61
Mar. 2018	$954.83	$295.94	$658.89	$5,965.15	$197,371.67
April 2018	$954.83	$296.93	$657.91	$6,623.06	$197,074.75
May 2018	$954.83	$297.91	$656.92	$7,279.97	$196,776.83
June 2018	$954.83	$298.91	$655.92	$7,935.89	$196,477.93
July 2018	$954.83	$299.90	$654.93	$8,590.82	$196,178.02
Aug. 2018	$954.83	$300.90	$653.93	$9,244.75	$195,877.12
Sept. 2018	$954.83	$301.91	$652.92	$9,897.67	$195,575.21
Oct. 2018	$954.83	$302.91	$651.92	$10,549.59	$195,272.30

When you secure a loan, the bank also gives you an amortization schedule like the one above. It is about 10 pages long and shows you each payment due over the course of the loan and what the principal/interest breakdown is inside of each payment. The amount you pay remains the same but what that money goes towards changes every month.

An amortization schedule is a hard pill to swallow when we look under the hood. Let's use the same house scenario from above to outline a hypothetical amortization schedule. In our example we're borrowing $200,000 at a 4% interest rate for 30 years to keep it simple. When we plug this into the amortization schedule you begin to see the disheartening results. Your monthly payment amount is $955 but only

$288 of that money goes towards your principal balance. The rest is payment to the bank for lending you that money.

Eventually you do pay down that principal balance after 360 monthly payments but in this time, you'll have paid over $140,000 in interest. So you paid back $200,000 plus $140,000 for a total of $340,000 for that $200,000 loan. That's a lot of money for money and a looooong time to wait to own your own house. The good news is that by the time we've colonized Mars you'll have this house paid off.

About That Payment

Most homeowners only pay attention to their monthly payment when they secure a mortgage. They ask themselves "Can I afford that monthly payment?" thinking very little of what that payment will amount to in the long run. This is normal human thinking but a short sighted and very expensive mistake.

You may think "Hey, my spouse and I earn $5,000 a month in combined income and our 30 year mortgage monthly payment is $2,500 so we're doing great!" But look at the scenario we just discussed: $140,000 in interest payments above the $200,000 you initially borrowed is A LOT. That is $140,000 you could have done oh so much more with!

The bank is making off like a bandit. We aren't making the case that they shouldn't. They assume a big risk in giving people large sums of money to purchase a home. But if you can cut down the amount of money you pay for money, shouldn't you try?

Of course you should try!!

Personally, we care much less about the monthly payment than we care about the amount of payments over the course of the loan. When we're done with you, you're never going to look at your monthly payment the same way again. We do this by attacking principal with our payments strategically. We're getting there.

How Taxes and Insurance Change Your Monthly Payments

There is no getting around property taxes. It is simply a part of owning real estate. The same goes for insurance. Taxes and insurance are often bundled into your monthly mortgage payment. The bank takes the estimated property tax, adds it with your yearly insurance bill, and pads that number. The law allows them to collect ⅙ more than what they estimate this cost to be. They divide that number by 12 and add that to your monthly payment. Then when the tax and insurance bill comes in, your mortgage company pays it for you.

The banks spin this as a simpler alternative than getting a yearly tax bill in the mail. Isn't that so kind of them? Who needs the extra headache of having to pay my tax bill separately? Take my money and hold it for me for a while. Great!

Not so fast. The bank takes your extra dollars and keeps them in an escrow account. When those bills are paid, they usually send you any money that is left over in the form of a check. This is handy if you are terrible at budgeting and will not be able to pay those bills when they come but if you are terrible at budgeting, why are you reading a book like this? Chances are that if you have picked up this book, you are pretty good with your money already and are ready for advanced personal finance tricks.

There are two reasons a bank would want to bundle your taxes and insurance with your mortgage payment:

1. You know the initialism CYA? Cover your...assets? That's what the bank is doing - covering their butts. If you do

not pay your property taxes, the city will take priority in a lien against the house (in most states). This means that if your house has to be sold at auction or foreclosed on, the city will get paid back first before the lender. The lender has no guarantee of ever being repaid in full. They get whatever scraps are left over from the emergency sale. The lender obviously doesn't like this option so they want to make double sure those taxes get paid!

2. They are also making money on your escrow account. Let me explain this. I am not a lender so I am not 100% sure that the lender earns interest on your escrow account, although my insurance agent assures me that they do. But I do know that they do not have to pay YOU any interest whatsoever so you could be keeping thousands of dollars in this account per year, earning ZERO on it. Plus, the bank is allowed to lend out money based on the money they have in house. If you put $100 in the bank, they are allowed to lend out $90 with interest. So of course they want to hang on to your money, if only for a little bit. This is the system of Fractional Reserve.

But isn't it YOUR money to save and earn interest on? Isn't it better to opt out of this escrow account if you are given the option? (Note: some lenders do not allow you to opt out.) My suggestion is that you have the discipline to save this money yourself, put it in an interest-bearing account, and then you'll have some extra dough left over to ease the pain of your tax bill.

Now that you understand the various components of a mortgage, take a look at your mortgage statement. How much have you paid in interest this year? How much have you paid down principal? This may be depressing but we are going to talk about how to dwindle those numbers down in a flash.

■ ■ ■

2

WHAT IS A HOME EQUITY LINE OF CREDIT?

In this chapter we're going to breakdown the benefits and mechanics of a home equity line of credit, or HELOC for short. The main thing you'll notice is how dramatically different a HELOC is from the traditional mortgage we deconstructed in Chapter 1. At the end of this chapter you'll understand how to structure your HELOC, how to find a great HELOC, and the one secret weapon that can dramatically shave years off your primary mortgage. Let's dive in!

What is a Home Equity Line of Credit?

Definition: A line of credit the bank extends to you based on the equity in your home and your credit history.

Think of a HELOC like any other bank product you are used to applying for: a home loan, a car loan, a student loan. The amount you get, the interest rate you secure, and the terms of the loan are based on your finances. Do you have good credit? Do you already have a lot of debt? Do you have a good job? All of these are factored into the final loan terms.

So you go to your bank and say, "I'd like to apply for a home equity line of credit please." Be sure to say please.

The banker will hand you an application. The application will ask you about all of the above questions and then ask for proof of your answers by way of bank statements, paystubs, drivers licenses, etc. Then the bank will run your credit. Obviously the higher the better.

Some good numbers to aim for here are a credit score of 660 or above, and a debt-to-income ratio of 45% or lower. This means that for all of the income you bring home, 45% or less of it goes to paying off debt. If too much of your paycheck is spoken for in debt payments, banks don't want anything to do with you. Who wants to get at the back of the line for creditors if they know that they won't get paid back? Many banks will look at anything under 36% debt as highly favorable. Make sure you know this number before you apply so you won't be embarrassed.

Now remember that your HELOC is based on the equity you own in your home. The equity is based on the amount your home is worth and the amount you owe. The bank offers to lend you a percentage of your equity. More about that later. What you need to know for starters is that in order to determine your home equity, the bank will need to appraise your home so they know what it is worth. They don't take your word for it. Everyone thinks they have the best house in the neighborhood. The bank needs proof. They want to know what the house could be sold at if you put it on the market today. Current market value.

The bank will assign an appraiser to your home. Sometimes they pay for this appraisal and sometimes they charge you back for it in the closing costs of the loan. Ask them about this when you apply.

Now that the bank has an appraisal that they trust, they can determine your equity. Let's stick with our scenario of a $200,000 house. The bank appraiser confirms that this is the current market value. Let's say that you still owe $150,000 on this house so your equity is $50,000.

A bank will give you a loan based on this equity because that equity is as good as cash if the home were sold. They will **not** give you a loan based on the entire value of the house. That would be taking out debt on your debt and even though this is America, we don't take debt quite that far. Your HELOC will be a percentage of the $50,000 equity that you would get out of your home sale. Most commonly, the loan will be between 70-90% of that equity. For simplicity sake let's assume an 80% loan of your $50,000 equity, which is $40,000.

So if all goes well, you've been approved for $40,000. Great! Now what?

Let's start with terms. If your credit is good and your debt is low, you can demand some great terms. Many banks offer a low introductory rate for the first year. My bank gives us a 1.99% interest rate for the first year. After that, the interest jumps to market rate. More about that later.

The typical HELOC is a 10 or 15 year loan. This is negotiable. You will make a monthly payment on this loan and you can choose interest only or an amortized payment which will knock down the principal of the loan. My HELOCs are interest-only and I will explain that more later.

Before we get to what you do with that money, let's first discuss two more tips about shopping for your HELOC.

Tip 1: Shop local.

We're not being idyllic here. Local banks can usually do much more for you than the large national chains can. We have a great relationship with our local bankers. They often waive bank fees for us with a few keystrokes just because we are sitting at their desks. They go to bat for us if the corporate office offers us terms we are not thrilled about. They give us lots of free pens. They tolerate our children playing the spin-until-you-fall-over game on their office chairs.

Local bankers also have a better understanding of your property value since they live in the same town. A national chain with a call center in another time zone will not be able to get an accurate sense of your home value. A banker that lives in your community will be much more comfortable in assessing your equity based on current market conditions.

Local banks usually have great incentives for you as well. They can't compete with the big chains without them. So look for low introductory interest rates, free checking and savings accounts, no-fee credit cards, and more.

Of course there are drawbacks of a local bank. They won't have nearly as many ATMs and their website and online banking will never be as robust as a Bank of America or Wells Fargo. That's just the way it goes. Personally, I'm glad to go without these bells and whistles for the low rates and fees.

My advice is to shop around between 3-4 banks, a few local and a few chains. See what each one can do for you and choose the most attractive player. What's that commercial that says that when banks compete, you win? It was probably a large banking corporation ironically enough but they were right!

Tip 2: Set up your HELOC like a checking account

Ask your bank if your HELOC can receive direct deposit. It should be easy to do but my banker did not know that a HELOC could do that until we did it. Let me explain.

A HELOC works like a checking account. Think about it, they've just extended you $40,000 worth of credit. You don't have to use it. It's up to you. They did not give you $40,000. They gave you the option to use $40,000.

How do you use it? With an account worth $40,000. You get an account number, a routing number, and possibly some checks and a debit card. The HELOC has a 0 balance when you open it. Say you spend $1,000. Now the HELOC has a $1,000 balance. You spend another $1,000. Now the HELOC has a $2,000 balance. The balance is what you have used of your original allotment.

So how do you pay that $2,000 back? We do this with direct deposit of the paycheck from our day jobs. Each week the entire paycheck goes into the HELOC to keep that balance moving back to 0. I'll explain more later but just know that keeping your HELOC in check and your money going exactly where you want it is much easier when your paycheck is filtered through your HELOC.

Our bank calls to verify each transaction out of our HELOC. This is a nice service to make sure that there is no fraud but can be kind of annoying if you use your HELOC for small purchases. So don't use it to buy Starbucks coffee. Use it for large purchases only. We're about to get into that right now so buckle up.

■ ■ ■

3

How To Play The Interest Game Like a Master

Interest and time are your two biggest enemies when it comes to a bank loan. This is important to keep in mind as you plan to attack your mortgage. Public enemy number one: Interest. Public enemy number two: time. Got it? Good. Let's plan our attack.

We've been over interest. It is simply the money you pay for money. The longer you spread those interest payments out, the more you are going to pay them to borrow this money. Why? Because the amount of interest you are paying is calculated each month based on what you have left to pay. Consider that the interest you are paying today is based on the principal balance. If you knock your principal balance down with big whacks, the time it takes to pay that mortgage back shrinks and so does the amount of interest you are paying.

We are talking about amortized interest here and amortization is an ugly beastly thing to calculate. But if you play around with an amortization calculator or spreadsheet you can see how the amount you are committed to paying in interest shrinks a TON when you put big payments in the "Extra Principal" column. This is because the amount of money you are paying for has been reduced. If you are paying 4% on $200,000, that is a much different story than paying 4% on $180,000. Get it?

The point I am trying to make here is that taking big chunks out of your principal balance with large payments is better than simply overpaying your mortgage little by little, month by month. Some people like to overpay their mortgage a little at a time each month for the same reason and that is great if that is all they can do. But if you want to accelerate and beat not only interest but also TIME, the math works out to take big swings at that principal balance as often as you can, rather than small bunts month-by-month.

That's where the HELOC comes in! If you've got a $40,000 HELOC and you put it on that $150,000 that you still owe the bank, it ALL goes towards principal! Now the interest you were set to pay for that $150,000 loan has just dropped by over $20,000, assuming a 4% interest rate on that loan!!! Holy cow! Not only that, the time you are set to pay back that loan dropped by almost 2 years. How good does that feel!?

But wait, you might be thinking, it's not like you still don't owe $150,000. Because now your original mortgage is worth $110,000 but you owe $40,000 to the HELOC so you still owe $150,000 in total to some kind of bank.

True! BUT the $40,000 is likely at a lower interest rate for at least a year. And you are paying simple interest on that loan rather than amortized interest.

Here is the thing to keep in mind: A home mortgage is paid for with amortized interest. A HELOC is paid for with simple interest. Up till this point we've been talking about amortized interest. Simple interest is determined by multiplying the daily interest-rate by the principal balance by the number of days that have elapsed between the payments you've made.

More simply (pun intended), simple interest is based on what you have borrowed and does not change depending on what is left on the loan. It is based on what you borrowed and agreed upon. So you are better off paying a loan with simple interest and knocking off the loan with amortized interest.

In fact, our general game plan is to take that HELOC and use it like a weapon. We swing it at every loan that we don't like in life: credit cards if we have high balances (which we generally don't but you get the idea), car loans, home loans. The HELOC is an awesome product. I want to switch it out for any bank products I have that are not awesome.

■ ■ ■

Of course a HELOC is not so awesome that it is free. We are going to talk about how you pay it down but not just yet. We want to first leave you with this visual that might help you make decisions about your HELOC.

Our kids love the teeter totter at the playground. Some call it a seesaw. Nuance. Anyway, you know this childhood game: one goes up and the other comes crashing down. One is lighter one is heavier. Paying down your primary mortgage is a lot like the teeter totter game. You put your two bank products on each side. Which one is heavier, meaning costs you more in interest? Which one is lighter, meaning costs you less? You want to destroy the heaviest one with the lightest one. Once you've done that, put your next heavy bank product on the opposing end and destroy that too. This is the true definition of leverage and it is a game the wealthy know how to play!

■ ■ ■

4

How to Pay Off Your HELOC

Using your HELOC like a checking account

So now you have a new loan in your name by way of a HELOC. And you want that loan paid off of course. How do you do that? It's time to get into the good stuff and show you how the secret sauce makes this all come together.

You could make payments to the HELOC every month with as much money as you can save up from your income. That's one way, sure. But we have another ninja trick way that works even better! Here's how it goes:

You tell your employer to put your entire paycheck into the HELOC as a direct deposit. Your HELOC is a bank account just like your checking account so why the heck not? So that HELOC gets ALL of your money that you make every month. And of course the balance will go down, down, down because you are doing this.

Wait, you say, how will I buy groceries? Pay my actual mortgage bill? Cell phone bill? Etc.!?

Good question! You pay it out of the HELOC. And if you spend less money than you made this month, the remaining balance will sit in the HELOC and dwindle that balance down to 0 before you know it.

So let's run a scenario. You have a $40,000 HELOC. You put $40,000 on your mortgage principal so that HELOC has a $40,000 balance. You make $10,000 per month. You direct deposit all of that $10,000 into your HELOC so the HELOC now has a $30,000 balance.

Now, your monthly expenses are $8,000. You pay for them out of the HELOC so now your principal balance is $38,000. So in one month, you have paid your HELOC down by $2,000. Do this WHOLE THING OVER next month and the HELOC balance is now $36,000. Do this for 18 months and your HELOC is down to 0!

But in 18 months, your introductory interest rate on that HELOC may be pretty high. Good point but the equity in your house is higher now, right? Renegotiate a new HELOC! Remember the HELOC was based on your equity of $50,000. But now you have equity of $100,000 so you are eligible for more money at a new low rate. So now you can do the same thing over again! Do it!

Let's continue to play this out because it is exciting. Now you have a HELOC for $80,000. You swing that at your principal balance of $100,000. You pay the $80,000 back $2,000 at a time. The HELOC is back to 0 in 40 months or a little over 3 years. So in under 5 years, you have paid off $130,000 of your mortgage and now have a $20,000 balance! Holy moly!!

So you take out a new HELOC for only $20,000 because you're being conservative. You pay that back in 10 months. Now you have NO mortgage! You have paid off your home mortgage in 68 months or a little over 5 years! As opposed to 30 years!!! How amazing does that feel!?

Now before you celebrate, keep in mind that the key here is that you spend less than you make every single month. You have to have money left at the end of the month, not month left at the end of the money. Every dollar you do not spend pays down your HELOC so that you can pay down your mortgage faster and faster.

Earlier we asked you to shop around for a bank that will let you use your home-equity line of credit as a checking account complete with a debit card, checkbook, and the ability to make deposits. I'm willing to bet that every month your normal checking account has a few hundred dollars left over just sitting there doing nothing. That money is not in the stock market, it's not in your 401(k). It's just sitting there in your checking account basically doing nothing. With our new strategy you're going to use that monthly leftover cash like a heat seeking missile to pay down our home-equity line of credit.

Now about those daily expenses like your daily latte or commuter train pass. Can you pay for those from your HELOC? You can but it can get tedious. Instead, we recommend paying for EVERYTHING with a low-interest, high-benefit credit card. Then you pay this credit card IN FULL every month with your HELOC. This way the bank does not call you to authorize every purchase out of your HELOC like our bank does. It would get annoying to have to authorize a charge from Dunkin Donuts every day. But also, you rack up points on every purchase with the card of your choice. Shop around for the best card you can get on Bankrate.com. We have paid for almost all of our travel using this strategy because we spend everything on the card and reap all the benefits. It's awesome!

There are other benefits of using a credit card for your expenses:

1. The security: Debit cards don't offer the same level of security as a credit card. Every transaction is protected by Visa, Mastercard, or American Express. Erroneous transactions can easily be removed from your account if you notice some fowl play. Additionally these cards offer car insurance and other protections when you use their services. You don't get that with an ATM card.

2. The Rewards: Disney vacations, airline miles, cash back, you name it there's a card that will make you happy!

3. Improved Credit Score: An ancillary benefit of using credit card and paying it off every month is that you're dramatically improving your credit score. Banks love to see that you are using their services and paying them back on time. Having an improved credit score will also help you when you want to renegotiate the terms of your HELOC at a future date. You may even get a lower interest rate thanks to your improved credit score.

Use the card for everything

Our ATM cards are only used when we need cash. Or at Costco because Costco doesn't accept credit cards for some odd reason. For everything else, we use our credit cards. Trips to Home Depot, Netflix, breakfast at the diner, and dry cleaning. You name it and it goes on the credit card. Remember that all of these transactions get paid off each month with a check from the HELOC. You might still get a phone call from the bank to verify the transaction but one phone call is better than 30.

Does this take discipline? Of course it does! This entire strategy takes discipline but this is an advanced personal finance technique and you would not have made it this far if you were not a disciplined person.

Part of this discipline is to set a goal to reduce your monthly expenses as much as possible. You don't have to go crazy but if you eat out six times a month try to cut that down to just four. That might save you $150 a month and because that additional cash is sitting in your HELOC account it's reducing your overall HELOC balance. Set a goal to live a certain percentage less than you've currently been living. We set a goal to eat meals at home more often and that brought down our monthly expenses.

Be honest with yourself and budget for all of your monthly expenses. Taking a few hours and tallying up every monthly item you spend can be eye opening. When we did this, we discovered a few internet subscription services that we were paying for that we'd totally forgotten and were no longer using. That extra $60 a month helped pay off our HELOC. By making a few small changes you will more quickly slice and dice your mortgage.

Remember, every dollar you don't spend helps pay down your HELOC, which helps pay down your mortgage. That is a powerful motivator not to overspend because it brings you that much closer to being free of the biggest loan in your name, your mortgage! The biggest monkey on your back, we're willing to bet!

■ ■ ■

5

How To Tie It All Together

You probably have a bunch of questions and numbers swirling around your head. Don't worry because now we're going to tie it all together in one complete package so you can see it in action. Let's do this as a list of Action Items so that you can get this done from start to finish.

1. Shop for a HELOC. Go to at least a few local banks. Research a few big banks too, as well as the bank that holds your mortgage currently. Introduce yourself to the banker and ask some questions about this product such as:
   o What are your introductory rates for a HELOC?
   o What do they normally lend on a HELOC? 80% the value of equity? 90%
   o Do they have fees associated with the HELOC such as check fees or ATM card fees?

- o Do they allow direct deposit of paychecks into the HELOC?
- o Do they require you to open a checking account in order to secure a HELOC?

2. Fill out the application and schedule the appraisal.
   - o The bank will want all sorts of financial documents: tax returns, pay stubs, bank statements. Be ready to gather those up. Thank goodness for paperless statements!
   - o The banker will call you when the appraisal is done and tell you what they think your home is worth. If you dispute this, tell them so! Ask of the appraiser was local. Ask what data they used to come up with this appraisal. This will determine your equity so you want a high value that is fair market value. Key word here is fair!

3. Discuss your equity and loan with the banker. They usually tell you that based on your income, equity, and home value, they can offer you X amount. I have never tried negotiating this amount but it couldn't hurt. If it works for you, let me know!

4. Go to the bank and sign closing documents! The bank is putting a second note on your house so you have to sign papers acknowledging this. That means that if something were to happen and you stopped paying all of your bills and the house was sold by the city, the bank would get paid back. Not first! The city always gets paid back first if there are back taxes. The next to take their money would be your primary mortgage company, and then the bank that offers you the HELOC. Signing for a HELOC is like a mini-mortgage session. It does not take NEARLY as long. We've done it in about 20 minutes. When you leave, the bank

gives you your account number and maybe some checks. And you're off!

5. Make the payment to your primary mortgage! Make sure you pay all of it to principal! If you don't mark it for principal the bank could think you're making at least part of it for a regular payment and take interest out of it. You're not paying interest with this money! You are REDUCING your interest burden with this money. Make this payment to PRINCIPAL ONLY. Check and double check that you do this correctly.

6. Now that you have a principal balance on your HELOC, schedule direct deposit of your paycheck into the HELOC account. You cannot deposit money into that account if there is no balance. We made the mistake of scheduling direct deposit into our HELOC before we had taken money out of it and the paycheck was returned. That was stressful. Use the money first before you try to pay it back.

7. Now see what happens to the length of your loan and the overall interest of your loan!! Watch it shrivel and shrink! So exciting!! I keep an amortization spreadsheet on my computer to show me what happens to these numbers every time I make a large payment to principal. Oh man does that feel good!!

8. Set and stick to your household budget. Set your bills to be paid through your credit card and pay off the credit card every month out of your HELOC.

9. Watch as your HELOC balance goes down with every paycheck, goes back up slightly to cover your expenses, and then down again with the next paycheck. Remember, every dollar you do NOT spend is the amount that pays off your HELOC and gets you closer to taking another whack out of your mortgage. Be disciplined!

10. Bonus step: Take a fun vacation with the points you rack up on your credit card! Tag us on social media so we can see it too!

Does this strategy work for everyone? No of course not! Here are a couple of reasons it may not work smoothly for you:

- You have bad credit and the bank won't loan to you;
- You are upside down in equity of your home;
- You cannot stick to a budget and commit to spending less than you make.

We can't help you fix those things overnight but all of them are fixable! This HELOC strategy is something to aim for once those things are under control.

For the rest of you with a steady job, decent credit, equity in your home, and the desire to beat the bank, this strategy is for you! We paid off a mortgage with a $294,000 balance in less than two years with this strategy. We opened a very expensive bottle of wine to celebrate! We'd love for you to be able to do the same.

Now go forth, pay off that mortgage! And write to us about your credit card vacation and mortgage payoff wine so we can celebrate together!

■ ■ ■

CONCLUSION

We want to thank you for reading this book. Even if you never employ this HELOC strategy, we at least hope that this book has armed you with tools to better understand your home mortgage and personal finances in order to make better decisions at every turn. But of course we want you to be mortgage-free. We want you to use your money to build wealth, not pay down debt. We want you to thrive, not survive!

On our website, www.morrisinvest.com, we have blogs, videos, and podcasts about how to build wealth and live off of passive income in order to be truly free from the rat race. Being free of a mortgage is just one step towards financial freedom. Having monthly cash flow is another. We help investors buy rental real estate and set up their estates so that they can build legacy wealth for themselves and their families. We hope you will explore our content because we spend a lot of time making it to inspire other families like ours! Best of luck to you and yours from us and ours!

■ ■ ■

ABOUT THE AUTHORS

Clayton and Natali Morris met while working as TV news broadcasters. Clayton has been a news anchor for Fox News for over a decade and Natali has worked for CBS and NBC for most of her career.

In 2010 they started a family and got serious about building legacy wealth for their three children, Miles, Ava, and Eve. They podcast, write, and speak around the world about personal finance and financial empowerment in order to help other families like theirs employ the skills they have learned along the way to attain true financial freedom.

Connect with the authors at morrisinvest.com

www.ingramcontent.com/pod-product-compliance
Lightning Source LLC
Chambersburg PA
CBHW051304170526
45165CB00004B/1851